Take Care
of Yourself!

Shohreh Afshar

PAGE PUBLISHING, INC.
Conneaut Lake, PA

First originally published by Page Publishing 2020

ISBN 978-1-64701-811-5 (pbk)
ISBN 978-1-64701-812-2 (digital)

Printed in the United States of America

A Word with Parents and Educators

This book intends to provide a simple approach, in the form of a story, for communicating and educating children about their body. The educational material of this book can benefit a wide range of children from preschool to junior high school.

Availability and accessibility of appropriate educational resources are necessary, but successfulness and effectiveness of these resources have a direct relationship with the extent of participation of parents and educators. It goes without saying that awareness of a child's private space and respect for it begins with parents and educators. Only when this prerequisite is met, a positive and constructive collaboration becomes possible.

For most parents talking about private parts is awkward and uncomfortable. Still, it is necessary to openly talk about private space just the way we talk about avoiding fire or wearing a helmet when riding a bike. Surely, difficulty of an educational and preventive discussion is far less than the difficulty of repairing and supporting discussions needed after an abuse has taken place. It's also important that children find us welcoming and open to this kind of subject so they do not avoid talking, thinking that it makes us uncomfortable. These kinds of discussions become normal when parents have an active presence in a child's life and exchange thoughts and feelings on different subjects and occasions.

Creating a safe space for conversation about child safety, especially if it is through evoking curiosity, can help with effective absorption of important points.

May this book assist parents and educators in their efforts toward raising awareness and preventing all form of child abuse.

Shohreh Afshar

Acknowledgments

I wish to express my gratitude to Moira Thompson, my patient editor and friend, Shima Sattary for her inspiration, Anita Miettunen for her literary critique, and Corene Brown for her assistance with my research.

Thank you to Page Publishing team who made this book possible.

And to those who actively and responsibly participate in making the world a safer and happier place for children.

Helen was the kind and beloved teacher of a small kindergarten. She had energetic and curious children in her class who were all very fond of her.

The second week of school had just started. Helen, who would usually bring some books to class, entered that day with a big bag. The children right away guessed that something new and exciting was going to take place.

Once everyone sat down, Helen asked, "How are you today?"

The children answered, "Very well, thank you!"

She then said, "I know you are very keen to find out what's in my big bag, right?"

The children loudly replied, "Yeeeeeeeeeeees!"

Helen said, "You will know very soon because it is about the subject we are going to learn today."

The children excitedly asked, "What subject?"

Helen answered, "Today we are going to talk about **good feelings** and **bad feelings**."

One of the children asked, "Good feelings like what?"

Helen said, "Like when our mother hugs us."

The children took a pause to imagine Helen's example. The smiles that appeared on their faces showed that they had understood what she meant.

Helen said, "All right everyone. Now I want *you* to give me some examples of a good feeling."

Maryam said, "Eating a big ice cream!"

Another child said, "Winning a game!"

4

Other children also gave examples, and Helen nodded to all of them until one of them asked, "What is a bad feeling then?"

Helen answered, "It's like when someone pushes us, and we fall to the ground."

The children became silent again. It was obvious from their gaze that they were searching for other examples in their minds.

Daniel said, "Like when someone takes away our toys."

Other children added a few more examples, and Helen listened to them all. When everyone was quiet again, Maryam, who was impatiently peeping at Helen's big bag, asked, "Would you now tell us what is in that big bag?"

Helen, who adored her curious children, kindly assured her, "Maryam, we have to wait just a little bit more before we take a look at what's inside the bag."

Maryam nodded in agreement, "Okay."

Helen continued, "Well done everyone. Now that we know what good feelings and bad feelings are, let's talk about **good touches** and **bad touches**."

One of the children asked, "What is a good touch?"

Helen said, "A good touch makes us feel good, like when your mom combs your hair." She continued, "Now *you* give me examples of a good touch that comes to your mind."

Mitra said, "Like when Maryam and I hold hands and play."

Kevin added, "Like when my father puts me on his shoulders and spins."

Helen, with a big smile said, "Well done kids! Those were all good examples."

Mitra raised her hand and asked, "What is a bad touch then?"

Helen answered, "A bad touch makes us feel bad and uncomfortable."

One of the kids said, "Like when my uncle hugs and kisses me, and I feel bad."

Maryam quietly said, "Like when someone touches us, and we don't like it."

Helen said, "That's right Maryam. Your body belongs to you and no one should touch it. When someone touches our **private parts**, we feel very bad and uncomfortable."

Kevin asked, "What is a private part?"

Helen said, "Our body has different parts like ears, eyes, hands, feet and private parts. Private parts are those areas of our body that are covered by bathing suits."

The kids listened to every word. Then Helen took two dolls out of her bag, one boy and one girl, who had bathing suits on.

Helen held up the dolls and asked the children to point out the private body parts.

13

Once she was confident that the children understood the differences of all the body parts, she turned to them and said, "Well done! Now we need to learn a very **important rule** about your private parts."

Mitra asked, "What rule?"

Helen said, "The important rule is that no one should see or touch your private parts. Also, you should not see or touch someone else's private parts." She continued, "Sometimes though, it's all right if you let others touch your body, like when your mother bathes you or your doctor examines you in your parents' presence."

One of the children asked, "What should we do if someone tries to touch us in a bad way?"

Helen said, "When you are next to someone, man or woman, known or stranger, who makes you feel bad or uncomfortable, you must **trust your feelings**."

Maryam asked, "What should we do then?"

Helen answered, "You must do three things. Shout loud and firm **no**! Then get **away** safely and **tell** someone you trust as soon as possible!"

Mitra asked, "What if they don't listen?"
Helen answered, "Tell it to the next trusted person. Keep telling until someone listens."

Next, Helen took out a big sheet of paper, which had some photos on it, and showed it to the children.

She said, "The people in these photos are in my **trusted circle**. A trusted circle includes the friends and relatives you can trust."

Helen gave each child a sheet of paper with a few empty frames on it. She asked them to fill the frames with photos or names of their trusted people.

She continued, "Try to fill in at least three frames on your sheet and bring it to class tomorrow. These people form your trusted circle. Remember that you must talk to a member of your trusted circle whenever someone makes you feel bad or uncomfortable."

One of the children asked, "What if someone touches us in a bad way and says it's a secret?"

Today's subject:
How to take care of yourselves

Helen said, "It's important to know the difference between a **good secret** and a **bad secret**. A good secret makes us feel good and does not harm anyone. It is also eventually told, like when we plan a surprise birthday party for someone. This is a good secret, and we feel good to keep it." She continued, "But a bad secret harms us and makes us feel bad, like when we know that someone is bullied by his classmates, but we don't tell anyone to help him. Or when somebody touches our private parts and tells us that it's a secret, and we shouldn't tell anyone. These are all bad secrets that harm us or others."

Helen continued, "Remember, if someone touched or harmed you in any way, it's not your fault. Don't worry about telling your trusted circle. They *want* you to tell them so they can help you and also stop the bad person."

The class break time was coming. Helen once more repeated the main points for the children. The children also showed how much they had learned and how much better they would take care of themselves from that day on.

The End

In case of emergency, call 911. If you have questions or need to speak with someone, contact the **Childhelp National Child Abuse Hotline** via call, text, or chat. Serving the U.S. and Canada, the hotline is staffed 24 hours a day, 7 days a week with professional crisis counselors who—through interpreters—provide assistance in over 170 languages. The hotline offers crisis intervention, information, and referrals to thousands of emergency, social service, and support resources. All calls, texts and chats are confidential. Contact:

1(800)-4-A-CHILD (1-800-422-4453) or ChildhelpHotline.org

The **Childhelp Speak Up Be Safe** research-based child abuse prevention education curriculum is proven effective and used throughout the United States and in 18 other nations to teach students in grades PK-12 how to recognize, interrupt, and tell safe adults about abusive situations. To learn more, visit:

SpeakUpBeSafe.org

CPSIA information can be obtained
at www.ICGtesting.com
Printed in the USA
LVHW072047290722
724658LV00006B/12

3 1901 10065 7966

9 781647 018115